# POSITIVITY
## — FOR —
## EVERY DAY
## JOURNAL

Simple Tips and Guided Exercises
to Help You Look on the Bright Side

vie

POSITIVITY FOR EVERY DAY JOURNAL

This fully updated and revised edition copyright © Summersdale Publishers Ltd, 2023
First published as *The Little Book of Positivity* in 2015
Published as *Positivity for Every Day* in 2021

Text by Elanor Clarke, updated and revised by Holly Brook-Piper

An Hachette UK Company
www.hachette.co.uk

Vie Books, an imprint of Summersdale Publishers Ltd
Part of Octopus Publishing Group Limited
Carmelite House
50 Victoria Embankment
LONDON
EC4Y 0DZ
UK

www.summersdale.com

Printed and bound in the Czech Republic

ISBN: 978-1-80007-833-8

Substantial discounts on bulk quantities of Summersdale books are available to corporations, professional associations and other organizations. For details contact general enquiries: telephone: +44 (0) 1243 771107 or email: enquiries@summersdale.com.

This journal belongs to:

.....................................................................................................

Date of birth:

.....................................................................................................

Date:

.....................................................................................................

How I feel before embarking on this journey:

.....................................................................................................

.....................................................................................................

Completion date:

.....................................................................................................

How I feel now I have completed this journey:

.....................................................................................................

.....................................................................................................

# INTRODUCTION

Remaining positive about yourself and your
situation is key to your happiness. It can
seem hard to remain on an even keel when
life throws obstacles in your way: increasing
work, home and even social commitments can
seem to conspire to make us feel negative
and unable to cope. This book is packed
with easy-to-follow tips and inspirational
journal prompts that can help you to put
a positive spin on your situation and see
the good in everything. If, however, you
find that low mood has started to affect
your day-to-day life, it is recommended
that you seek advice from your doctor.

# HOW TO USE THIS JOURNAL

Journaling will be most effective if you do it regularly, so try to find a few moments to work through the prompts on the following pages every day. By making it a habit, you will discover positive thinking becomes a way of life instead of something you struggle to maintain. Be as detailed in your writing as you can; the more detailed your writing is, the greater the insight you will have into your thoughts, feelings and future.

Lastly, don't let anything hold you back – there is no right or wrong to what you write in this journal, it is yours alone so be honest with yourself and try not to censor your writing.

# MAKE A HAPPY LIST

In order to focus on the positive, try making
a list of all the good things in your life. This
might seem difficult at first, but you can always
ask friends and family for help. The list could
be made up of personal or general points,
for example "I am healthy" or "My family
is supportive." You can refer to this when
negativity seems to be creeping in and you need
to remind yourself of the good around you.

**Remind yourself of all the good around you by creating a list of the things that are going well in your life at the moment.**

- ......................................................................
- ......................................................................
- ......................................................................
- ......................................................................
- ......................................................................

Write a message to your future self, encouraging you to stay positive in times of adversity.

......................................................................

......................................................................

......................................................................

......................................................................

......................................................................

......................................................................

Use this space to write your own thoughts.

# WALK INTO POSITIVITY

Starting an exercise regime can be daunting, especially if you are feeling negative. Joining a gym or going to a group class can seem like the last thing you would want to do. However, exercise can be as simple as going for a walk. Just a half-hour walk each day can significantly improve your health and emotional well-being. You can fit this in on the way to work, at lunchtime or whenever feels right for you. Try going for walks in daylight, in natural surroundings; the sunlight will warm your skin and should make you feel more positive as it produces mood-boosting vitamin D.

To start your journey into exercising more, use the weekly planner below to add some additional movement to your daily routine.

|  | Exercise | Time | Location |
|---|---|---|---|
| MON | | | |
| TUE | | | |
| WED | | | |
| THU | | | |
| FRI | | | |
| SAT | | | |
| SUN | | | |

Once the week is completed, use the space below to document how the experience has benefitted your health and emotional well-being.

....................................................................................

....................................................................................

....................................................................................

....................................................................................

Use this space to write your own thoughts.

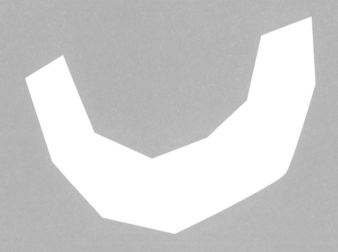

MY OPTIMISM
WEARS HEAVY BOOTS
AND IS LOUD.

Henry Rollins

# DANCE YOURSELF
# FIT AND HAPPY

Dancing is, for many people, one of the most
fun ways to get fit and move your body more.
Having fun, alongside releasing the mood-
boosting endorphins exercise provides, is a
great positivity cocktail. This can be as simple
as putting on your favourite music at home and
dancing around your living room or bedroom,
or you could try a class. Choose a dance style
that suits you and, above all, enjoy it.

**Write a list of your favourite pieces of music to dance to.**

- .....................................................................................
- .....................................................................................
- .....................................................................................
- .....................................................................................
- 

Have a go at dancing while no one is watching.
How did you feel while doing it?

.........................................................................................

.........................................................................................

.........................................................................................

.........................................................................................

Use the space below to come up with some other fun
fitness ideas for releasing mood-boosting endorphins.

.........................................................................................

.........................................................................................

.........................................................................................

.........................................................................................

Use this space to write your own thoughts.

# MODERATE YOUR ALCOHOL INTAKE

When feeling low or stressed after a difficult day, many people will reach for a drink to help them relax and unwind. Alcohol can be instantly calming, but this is negated by its depressant qualities and the feeling of anxiety that can be left behind once the effects wear off. Alcohol can also disturb your sleep, contrary to the purported benefits of a "nightcap", and feeling tired and anxious can cause negative thinking. Try to cut down your drinking as much as possible and, if you do have a drink, opt for a small glass of Chianti, Merlot or Cabernet Sauvignon, as the plant chemicals – called procyanidins – that are abundant in these particular wines are reasonably beneficial to health, especially cardiovascular health. These wines are also rich in melatonin, the sleep hormone, and a well-rested person is more likely to be a positive person.

Using some of your favourite flavours, create your very own alcohol-free beverage for a special occasion.

**Ingredients**

........................................................................

........................................................................

........................................................................

........................................................................

........................................................................

**Method**

........................................................................

........................................................................

........................................................................

........................................................................

........................................................................

What are the most effective ways that you find help you to relax and unwind?

........................................................................

........................................................................

........................................................................

**Use this space to write your own thoughts.**

# I CHOOSE POSITIVITY

# DE-STRESS YOUR HOME

Although you may not realize it, your living environment can become a stressor – whether that's because you have too much clutter around you, too many demands on your time and resources, or perhaps you don't feel comfortable in your home. Try reducing stress by using simple cleaning and decluttering methods. Make sure you only keep things you really need – unwanted clutter can be sold via websites such as eBay, or given to charity shops. When cleaning, start in one room and clean it from the back to the front. Divide the house room by room and tidy one each day, if that helps. These steps will make your home a more comfortable environment and increase your positive feelings about where you live, as well as helping you to stay on top of your chores.

Using the weekly planner below, pick a room a day to declutter. If items are no longer used or don't bring you pleasure, it's probably time to give them away.

| | Room to be decluttered |
|---|---|
| MON | |
| TUE | |
| WED | |
| THU | |
| FRI | |
| SAT | |
| SUN | |

What were the positives of decluttering?

......................................................................................................

......................................................................................................

Write down three things about your home that bring you joy.

1. ................................................................................................

2. ................................................................................................

3. ................................................................................................

**Use this space to write your own thoughts.**

# MAKE YOUR WORKSPACE CALM

The workplace is, for many of us, the most stressful environment we can find ourselves in. Workplace stress is often a source of concern for people and can leave us feeling very negative. To make your workplace feel calmer, try adding some plants to your desk area, as they not only brighten up the place and give you some of the calming benefits of nature but also help oxygenate the environment. It is equally important to make sure you take regular breaks from your work to avoid feeling overburdened, even if you just go to make a drink. Finally, avoid letting other people's stress rub off on you. Stress can be "caught", so if a colleague is complaining and being overly negative, either move the conversation away from the subject or, if you can't, excuse yourself and spend some time away from them.

**Come up with five adjectives to describe how you want your workspace to feel.**

What ways could you improve your workspace?

...........................................................................................

...........................................................................................

...........................................................................................

Come up with some ideas to help remind you to take a 5–10 minute break every hour. Try to implement them this week.

• ...........................................................................................

• ...........................................................................................

• ...........................................................................................

Describe how taking regular breaks benefits you.

...........................................................................................

...........................................................................................

...........................................................................................

**Use this space to write your own thoughts.**

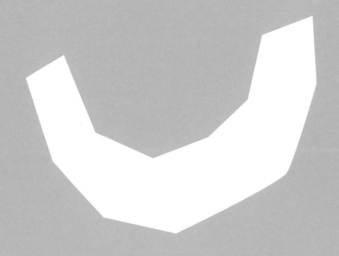

ACT AS IF WHAT
YOU DO MAKES
A DIFFERENCE.
IT DOES.

William James

# MAKE A BUDGET AND STICK TO IT

Financial worries are one of today's biggest stressors, with more and more people in increasing debt and/or out of work. Taking control of your finances is a great way to make you feel more positive as it helps to reduce the stress that can bring your mood down, and it shows that you can take on a difficult situation and improve it. One simple way to cut back on non-essential spending is to cancel any direct debits for services you do not want or need. Next, look at debt: make sure you are paying off the debts with the highest interest rates first, so you save money. Getting expert advice on your debts and how to manage them is a good idea, especially if you are not sure where to start. Finally, make sure you spend your disposable income on the things that are most important to you.

**Use this simple table to give you a rough overview of your expenditures every month.**

| Expense | Budget | Actual amount spent |
|---------|--------|---------------------|
|         |        |                     |
|         |        |                     |
|         |        |                     |
|         |        |                     |
|         |        |                     |
|         |        |                     |
|         |        |                     |

Are you able to make any cutbacks?

......................................................................

What is important to you personally to spend your disposable income on?

......................................................................

......................................................................

How does taking charge of your financial situation make you feel?

......................................................................

......................................................................

Use this space to write your own thoughts.

# UNDERSTAND YOUR STRESSORS

There are several broad issues that often cause stress in the majority of people, for example work pressures, relationship difficulties or financial problems. As individuals, we tend to know ourselves best and can work out which things affect us the most – these are known as "triggers" or "stressors". Identifying your triggers and making small, manageable changes are important steps in de-stressing. For example, it may be that driving to work makes you stressed, or maybe it's going for big nights out. In these instances, why not try getting the bus to work, or arranging smaller social gatherings with your friends?

Use the table below to identify some of your "triggers" and describe how they make you feel. Once you've identified what causes you stress and anxiety, come up with small, manageable changes to take control of these stressors.

| Trigger/stressor | How I feel | Coping strategy |
|---|---|---|
|  |  |  |
|  |  |  |
|  |  |  |

Describe how it feels taking control.

...........................................................................................

...........................................................................................

...........................................................................................

Use this space to write your own thoughts.

I CAN OVERCOME CHALLENGES THAT COME MY WAY

# AVOID "STICKY" SITUATIONS

It is likely that when you look at your triggers, certain situations or even people come up as major stressors. One of the best ways to remove stress is to avoid these people and situations wherever possible. Politely decline social situations that make you feel stressed; when you are feeling more positive, you could always confront those stressors and hopefully remove or reverse the effect they have on you. If it is someone close to you that is a stressor, why not sit down with them and have an honest conversation about how you are feeling. If it is a situation that is worrying you, try writing a list of what it is about that particular situation that is causing you stress and come up with some constructive potential solutions to overcome the problem.

**List three stressors in your life you would most like to confront.**

1.
.......................................................................................................
2.
.......................................................................................................
3.
.......................................................................................................

How would you go about confronting these stressors?

.......................................................................................................

.......................................................................................................

.......................................................................................................

.......................................................................................................

.......................................................................................................

.......................................................................................................

.......................................................................................................

Describe the scariest thing you have done
that turned out to be worth it.

.......................................................................................................

.......................................................................................................

.......................................................................................................

.......................................................................................................

.......................................................................................................

.......................................................................................................

Use this space to write your own thoughts.

# LOVE YOUR BEDROOM

Poor-quality sleep can have as much of an effect on your mood as lack of sleep. To help ensure that you feel great and ready to start the day each morning, make your bedroom into your personal sanctuary. Experts advise that bedrooms should be for sleep and sex only, so remove all distractions: do away with the computers and televisions, and even, if you can, your mobile phone. If you would usually use your mobile as an alarm, try investing in an alarm clock to help you keep technology out of the bedroom. Maintain a paperwork-free zone by opening your post elsewhere and save important discussions for other rooms. Finally, make sure your space is tidy and inviting, and soon you will be sleeping soundly and feeling more positive from the moment you wake up.

**Write down three of your favourite things about your bedroom.**

1. ..............................................................................................

2. ..............................................................................................

3. ..............................................................................................

Jot down some ideas for actions you could take to turn your bedroom into a more peaceful sanctuary.

- ..............................................................................................

- ..............................................................................................

- ..............................................................................................

- ..............................................................................................

- 

Try making a couple of the above changes and in the space below describe how they have increased your positivity.

..............................................................................................

..............................................................................................

..............................................................................................

**Use this space to write your own thoughts.**

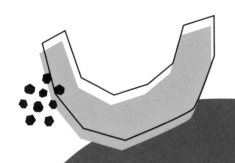

GO CONFIDENTLY
IN THE DIRECTION
OF YOUR DREAMS.
LIVE THE LIFE
YOU'VE IMAGINED.

Henry David Thoreau

# CLEANLINESS FOR POSITIVITY

We all feel good when we're fresh from the bath or shower, and keeping that fresh feeling in the bedroom helps to improve sleep and keep us positive. Bed linen that is freshly washed will feel cool and comforting against the skin. It is important to wash your sheets once a week, or more often if you have been unwell or if the weather is particularly hot. If you have the chance to, try air-drying your sheets on a line for added freshness.

Sometimes the most difficult part of keeping on top of chores, such as changing bedding, is knowing when and where to begin. Using the checklist below to get you started, make a note of chores to be completed this week.

**Monday**

☐                               ☐

**Tuesday**

☐                               ☐

**Wednesday**

☐                               ☐

**Thursday**

☐                               ☐

**Friday**

☐                               ☐

**Saturday**

☐                               ☐

**Sunday**

☐                               ☐

Describe how keeping on top of chores has boosted your positive mindset.

**Use this space to write your own thoughts.**

# LESS SCREEN TIME, MORE SLEEP

Most of us spend ever-increasing amounts of time in front of screens each day – computers, tablets, televisions and smartphones are core parts of most people's lives. These sorts of backlit screens, however, are detrimental to our sleep cycles. It may seem like watching a film or reading an article on your tablet is a good way to unwind before bed, but these activities make the brain more alert, and therefore make it harder to switch off at night. Bright screens halt the production of the sleep hormone, melatonin, in a similar way to daylight. Instead, try reading a book in gentle light, or listening to some calming music to help you drift off.

**Write a list of books you want to read.**

.................................................................................................

.................................................................................................

.................................................................................................

.................................................................................................

**Write a list of any pieces of music that you find relaxing.**

.................................................................................................

.................................................................................................

.................................................................................................

.................................................................................................

Try reading a book or listening to calming music the next time you go to bed. When you wake in the morning, use the space below to describe how it benefitted your bedtime routine and positively affected your sleep.

.................................................................................................

.................................................................................................

.................................................................................................

.................................................................................................

.................................................................................................

.................................................................................................

# Use this space to write your own thoughts.

I AM
WORTHY
OF WHAT
I DESIRE

# INVEST IN SOME ME TIME

It is all too easy to believe that all your time should be spent doing "useful" things, or being there for other people. This is, however, not true. Trying to keep going all the time for the sake of others, without giving yourself the space to enjoy your own company, will leave you feeling drained and tired, allowing negativity to creep in. For a positivity boost, try taking the night off. Indulge in your favourite foods, watch a film or series that you love, pick up a book you've been meaning to read and, most importantly, switch off from the rest of the world. Perhaps you want to pamper yourself, too, giving your feet a soak or indulging in an extra-long bath. You will likely feel all the more positive for giving your batteries a chance to recharge.

**Envisage your perfect "me day" to boost your positivity. In the space below, write down what it would involve.**

Morning

....................................................................................................

....................................................................................................

Afternoon

....................................................................................................

....................................................................................................

Evening

....................................................................................................

....................................................................................................

Describe the physical and mental benefits you experience when taking time for yourself.

....................................................................................................

....................................................................................................

Below, set yourself a self-care goal to make recharging your batteries a part of your weekly routine.

....................................................................................................

....................................................................................................

Use this space to write your own thoughts.

# LOOK AFTER YOUR SKIN

Healthy-looking skin is often the basis for feeling good about your looks. Seeing someone healthy when you look at yourself in the mirror can give you a boost and make you feel more positive. To keep your skin in the best shape, make sure you cleanse and moisturize regularly. You don't need to buy expensive products, just ensure that the product is designed for your skin type: whether dry, oily, combination or normal. Remember to wear sunscreen. Even when the weather isn't warm, the rays of the sun can cause damage and age your skin, so it's important to select one with a high SPF and good UVA and UVB protection. Getting a little time in the sun, however, is good for you. Up to 15 minutes without suncream will not only feel great on your skin, but will also help to boost your vitamin D and serotonin levels, which in turn improves mood.

Sometimes, remembering to moisturize is half the battle. Use this daily table to help remind you.

|  | Morning ✓ | Evening ✓ |
|---|---|---|
| Monday |  |  |
| Tuesday |  |  |
| Wednesday |  |  |
| Thursday |  |  |
| Friday |  |  |
| Saturday |  |  |
| Sunday |  |  |

Are there any other self-care regimes you want to incorporate into your life?

...................................................................

...................................................................

...................................................................

In the space below, describe how you can go about making these changes.

...................................................................

...................................................................

...................................................................

Use this space to write your own thoughts.

MAY YOU LIVE
EVERY DAY
OF YOUR LIFE.

Jonathan Swift

# DRESS THE WAY YOU WANT TO

Having a wardrobe that reflects your personality and style can help boost your positivity. Start by decluttering your current wardrobe so you are left with your basics and favourites. Get rid of anything too old, especially if it does not fit or doesn't make you feel good. These clothes don't have to go to waste; they can be sold online through websites such as eBay, or taken to a local charity shop. When selecting new items, choose well-fitting clothes that reflect your personality and where you want to be in your life. Make sure that when you look in the mirror, what you are wearing makes you think "Yes, I look good today," rather than "What am I wearing?" or "It will have to do." Feeling good in your clothes will make you feel more comfortable in yourself and boost your self-image.

**Write a list of the times or occasions when you felt confident in what you wore.**

. . . . . . . . . . . . . . . . . . . . . . . . . . . . . . . . . . . . . . . . . . . . . . . . . . . . . . . . . . . . . . . . . . . . . . . .

. . . . . . . . . . . . . . . . . . . . . . . . . . . . . . . . . . . . . . . . . . . . . . . . . . . . . . . . . . . . . . . . . . . . . . . .

In the space below, describe how feeling good in your clothes has a positive impact on how you feel about yourself.

. . . . . . . . . . . . . . . . . . . . . . . . . . . . . . . . . . . . . . . . . . . . . . . . . . . . . . . . . . . . . . . . . . . . . . . .

. . . . . . . . . . . . . . . . . . . . . . . . . . . . . . . . . . . . . . . . . . . . . . . . . . . . . . . . . . . . . . . . . . . . . . . .

Sketch your favourite outfit that gives you confidence.

Use this space to write your own thoughts.

# LAUGH MORE

It may seem simple, but the act of laughing makes people feel more positive. When you laugh out loud, natural endorphins are released, which give you feelings of happiness. Laughter is also good for you, helping to keep your blood pressure steady and improving your sleep. Try watching your favourite comedy or getting together for a good laugh with friends or family for a positivity lift. Another way to bring laughter into your life could be laughing yoga (also known as laughter yoga). This is a popular movement with the main aim of relieving stress using a combination of breathing techniques and laughter exercises to connect with your inner child.

**Use the space below to write down some of your favourite laugh-out-loud, happy memories.**

........................................................
........................................................
........................................................
........................................................
........................................................

Who never fails to make you laugh?
Write about a funny memory you share together.

........................................................
........................................................
........................................................
........................................................

Jot down some ways to bring more laughter into your life.

........................................................
........................................................
........................................................
........................................................

**Use this space to write your own thoughts.**

# I AM STRONG, CONFIDENT, AND IN CONTROL OF MY LIFE

# LEARN SOMETHING NEW

Learning is one of the best gifts you can give yourself, and learning something new can help with positivity in several ways. Firstly, new knowledge or skills will give your confidence a lift and make you feel more positive about your abilities. Secondly, if you attend a class, meeting people there is a great way to enhance your social life. Finally, learning something new gives you the opportunity to talk to your loved ones about your new experiences. What you choose to learn can be anything from a new language to drawing, and everything in between. Choose something which you think will enrich your life and, above all, enjoy it.

**In the space below, write down anything you'd love to learn how to do, or something you'd like to learn more about.**

- .............................................................
- .............................................................
- .............................................................
- .............................................................
- .............................................................

What are your motivations for learning something new and how might you benefit from this new skill?

.............................................................

.............................................................

.............................................................

.............................................................

Reflect on a time when learning something new has enriched your life and describe it in the space below.

.............................................................

.............................................................

.............................................................

.............................................................

# Use this space to write your own thoughts.

# WALK A DOG

It is well known that spending time with animals can boost your mood. Dog walking is a positive experience for you and the pet, giving you both the chance for some green exercise. If you don't have a dog of your own, you could offer to walk a friend or family member's animal. As well as giving you the opportunity to get out into nature and share that with a furry companion, it will free up time for your friend or family member to do more for themselves. Studies have shown that doing kind and helpful things for others can boost serotonin levels, improving your mood and overall well-being. It's a win-win situation!

**Write a list of mood-boosting activities that you could try outside of your home or work.**

- .................................................
- .................................................
- .................................................

- .................................................
- .................................................
- .................................................

Try to complete at least one of these mood boosters every day for a week.

| | Mood-boosting activity | ✓ |
|---|---|---|
| MON | | |
| TUE | | |
| WED | | |
| THU | | |
| FRI | | |
| SAT | | |
| SUN | | |

In the space below, describe how introducing daily mood boosters positively affected your productivity and mindset.

.................................................

.................................................

# Use this space to write your own thoughts.

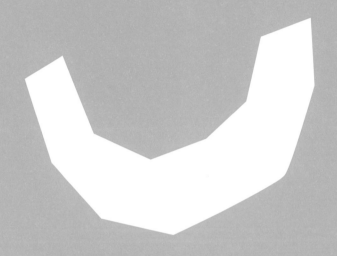

FALL DOWN
SEVEN TIMES,
STAND UP EIGHT.

Japanese proverb

# SPEAK WITH POWER

When you feel negative, it can come across in the way you speak. Worry may cause your voice to become high-pitched as your vocal cords tighten. You may also end up speaking in a way that lacks authority. This can cause a vicious circle of self-doubt, as you may not feel listened to or respected. To improve this situation, try speaking with power: let your tone be deeper, and keep your words slow and steady. Say what you want to say, like you mean it, and see the difference it can make. If you try this in front of a mirror it can be even more helpful, as you get used to seeing yourself talk. Seeing yourself progress to speaking calmly and with power can help you to overcome nerves the next time you have a challenging conversation or have to speak up in a group or work setting.

Create some positive statements that apply
to your life to help build your confidence.
Read these out loud to yourself every day.

- I can
- I will
- I am
- I can
- I will
- I am

In the space below, describe the difference
saying these positive statements daily has
had on your self-esteem and self-belief.

Use this space to write your own thoughts.

# GET TOGETHER WITH FRIENDS AND FAMILY

Having a get-together with friends and family is good for everyone involved. You could host and arrange for a group of people to come to your place for a movie night where each person could pick their favourite film, or invite people round for a meal where everyone brings a different dish. Take the time to catch up with everyone and see how they are doing, let yourself be the gracious host and be there for your friends, whether they need to talk, need a shoulder to cry on or just require some good company. Vary your get-togethers depending on your guests' interests.

**Create a list of ideas for get-togethers with friends and family.**

- ....................................................................................................................
- ....................................................................................................................
- ....................................................................................................................
- ....................................................................................................................
- ....................................................................................................................

Reflect on a time when your friends have been there to support you and how it made you feel.

....................................................................................................................

....................................................................................................................

....................................................................................................................

....................................................................................................................

....................................................................................................................

Write a list of people you would like to reach out to.

- ....................................................................................................................
- ....................................................................................................................
- ....................................................................................................................
- ....................................................................................................................
- ....................................................................................................................

Use this space to write your own thoughts.

I HAVE
THE POWER
TO CHANGE
MY LIFE

# WRITE A LETTER

Most of us have relatives or friends who live at the other end of the country, or have even moved abroad. Give yourself and them a boost by sitting down to write a letter by hand, letting them know what you've been up to and asking them plenty of questions. Use this as an opportunity to catch up in a way you wouldn't be able to over the phone or via Facebook, by being honest and open, and perhaps sending a little memento such as a photograph along with your note.

Use the space below to draft a letter to a friend or member of your family that you would normally only be in touch with infrequently or through social media. Use this as an opportunity to express your feelings and ask questions about how things are for them.

Dear                              ,

Use this space to write your own thoughts.

# VOLUNTEER LOCALLY

Charities and voluntary organizations are always in need of help. Why not use some of your spare time to help out at a local animal rescue centre or charity shop, or even give out leaflets? You can get in touch with charities easily through their websites and they will let you know where they need help most. Using your time constructively and helping a charitable cause is a great way to make you feel more positive about yourself, and about the way you use your free time, while spreading a little positivity as well.

**Use the space below to answer the following questions:**

Write about a time when someone has helped you and how it made you feel.

.......................................................................................

.......................................................................................

.......................................................................................

How did you show your gratitude?

.......................................................................................

.......................................................................................

.......................................................................................

Is there an organization that could currently use your help?

.......................................................................................

.......................................................................................

.......................................................................................

Research local charities and in the space below, write any important details you find.

.......................................................................................

.......................................................................................

.......................................................................................

**Use this space to write your own thoughts.**

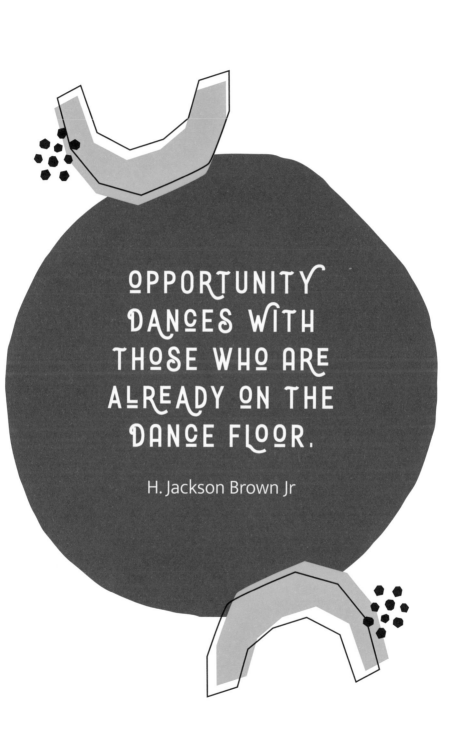

OPPORTUNITY
DANCES WITH
THOSE WHO ARE
ALREADY ON THE
DANCE FLOOR.

H. Jackson Brown Jr

# KNOW A THOUGHT

Each of us will have as many as 50,000 thoughts every day. These can be simple things, such as "What should I watch tonight?", or they can be powerful, such as "I'm not a good enough partner." Part of the concept of mindfulness – a practice that focuses on the moment, helping you to recognize your thoughts and actions – is understanding that thoughts are simply thoughts. They have no substance and do not need to control the way you feel and behave. Repeating the same negative thought pattern for many years may have had a detrimental effect on your emotional state, leaving you feeling negative and drained. Once you can recognize this negativity as simply a thought, you can begin to challenge it and rebuild your sense of self.

**Write down two self-defeating thoughts that have a detrimental effect on your emotional well-being.**

1.

....................................................................................................................

....................................................................................................................

2.

....................................................................................................................

....................................................................................................................

Reframe these thoughts in a positive way and in
the space below write them down. Explain how
they make you stronger and encourage you instead
of being damaging to your self-confidence.

....................................................................................................................

....................................................................................................................

....................................................................................................................

....................................................................................................................

....................................................................................................................

....................................................................................................................

....................................................................................................................

....................................................................................................................

....................................................................................................................

....................................................................................................................

....................................................................................................................

**Use this space to write your own thoughts.**

........................................................................

........................................................................

........................................................................

........................................................................

........................................................................

........................................................................

........................................................................

........................................................................

........................................................................

........................................................................

........................................................................

........................................................................

........................................................................

........................................................................

........................................................................

........................................................................

........................................................................

........................................................................

# TRY POSITIVITY MANTRAS

A mantra, or affirmation, is a phrase that you repeat
to yourself. Mantras can be thought or said out loud.
Many people believe that actually saying your mantra
makes it more effective, as vocalizing something
gives it more substance. You can also write your
chosen mantra down and put it somewhere you
are likely to see it, such as the kitchen or bathroom.
Choose your mantra based on what is important
to you, not what you feel others will accept; it
could be anything, from "I will pass my exam" to "I
am a good, honest person." Regularly repeating
your chosen mantra will help you reaffirm
your faith in yourself and your abilities.

Create some of your own positive mantras to repeat
to yourself to reaffirm your faith in your abilities.
If you need inspiration, take a look at some of the
positive mantras dotted throughout this book.

- ................................................................................
- ................................................................................
- ................................................................................
- ................................................................................
- ................................................................................
- ................................................................................
- ................................................................................
- 

In the space below, write what positive impacts
you want these mantras to have on your life.

................................................................................

................................................................................

................................................................................

................................................................................

................................................................................

................................................................................

Use this space to write your own thoughts.

# I AM
## ENOUGH

# BE HAPPY WITH YOU

Perfectionism can be destructive; continually striving for a perceived version of perfection can stop you from being happy with who you already are and from seeing all the positive things you have already achieved. One of the most common perfectionist tendencies is to compare yourself with others. This may take the form of direct comparison, such as "Viresh is more successful at work than I am" or of general comparison along the lines of "I wish I could be more like Lily." Either way, in seeing others as somehow better than you, you are moving your focus away from your positives. In trying to be like other people, you stop yourself from being the best version of you. Try instead to think about what areas of your life you would like to improve and work on those areas without comparing with others, while also recognizing your strong points.

**Recognize your strengths by answering the following statements:**

My greatest strengths are:

.........................................................................................

.........................................................................................

What I love most about myself is:

.........................................................................................

.........................................................................................

What makes me a good person is:

.........................................................................................

.........................................................................................

Identify two areas in your life you'd like to improve. Beside each one, write down the first steps you could take to making the changes you need to feel content with your life.

1.
.........................................................................................

.........................................................................................

2.
.........................................................................................

.........................................................................................

Use this space to write your own thoughts.

# BE POSITIVELY ASSERTIVE

It can sometimes seem easier to say "yes" rather than "no", even if you are really not happy with a situation. This can lead to negativity towards yourself for giving in and to others for "making" you do things you don't want to. You need to realize that your own needs are as important as everybody else's. Consider these simple scenarios: your boss asks you to take on a new project when you are already overworked. Instead of taking it on, you could explain the situation to your boss, so that a solution can be found. Your friend asks you to go out, but what you really want to do is to stay at home and read a book. Instead of going out to please your friend, you could let them know that you are not in the mood. The likelihood is that they will appreciate your honesty.

Concentrating on what is important to you and your life, use the table below to explore your life goals.

| Top life goals | Your motivation for achieving these goals | Your first steps towards achieving these goals |
|---|---|---|
| 1 | | |
| 2 | | |
| 3 | | |

Use this space to write your own thoughts.

YOU'RE THE
BLACKSMITH
OF YOUR OWN
HAPPINESS.

Swedish proverb

# TALK TO FRIENDS AND FAMILY

When trying to better understand any subject, talking to other people can prove invaluable, and the topic of how to stay positive is no different. As this is a personal subject, ask your friends and family how they stay positive, or how they deal with negative feelings, and what their coping mechanisms are; you may be surprised by their answers. Getting a broad picture by asking people you trust to share their views and experiences can help you better understand how to achieve a positive mindset.

**Approach a friend or family member and ask them the following questions. Write their answers in the spaces provided.**

How do you stay positive?

......................................................................................................................

......................................................................................................................

......................................................................................................................

How do you handle negative feelings?

......................................................................................................................

......................................................................................................................

......................................................................................................................

What are your coping mechanisms for difficult situations?

......................................................................................................................

......................................................................................................................

......................................................................................................................

Reflecting on their responses, how do you feel about how you deal with negative emotions?

......................................................................................................................

......................................................................................................................

......................................................................................................................

Use this space to write your own thoughts.

# BE YOUR OWN GUIDE

Self-guided meditation can be an excellent starting point for understanding how you view events – both positive and negative – and how they affect you. Meditation comes in many forms and, in this exercise, you are your own guide. Sit in a comfortable position, or lie down if you prefer, and close your eyes. Think of an event in your life that has negative feelings attached to it. Try to relive this event in your mind, without judgement, while you focus on the emotions and thoughts that it stirs up. Throughout, be non-judgemental; simply allow thoughts and feelings to come up, and recognize them for what they are. Next, do the same for a positive, happier event. For both, try to immerse yourself in the sounds, smells and sights around you. This will help you to understand what has triggered positive and negative emotions.

**Relive an event that has negative emotions attached to it. Describe your feelings surrounding it.**

......................................................................................

......................................................................................

How have these negative emotions affected you?

......................................................................................

......................................................................................

Relive an event that has positive emotions attached to it. Describe your feelings surrounding it.

......................................................................................

......................................................................................

How have these positive emotions affected you?

......................................................................................

......................................................................................

Reflect upon what has triggered the negative and positive emotions in these situations.

......................................................................................

......................................................................................

**Stop if reliving these experiences becomes too overwhelming.**

**Use this space to write your own thoughts.**

I CAN BE
ANYTHING
I WANT
TO BE

# KEEP A DIARY

Many people find keeping a diary cathartic
as it provides a structured way to discuss and
release emotions, as well as acting as a record
of your recent history, which you can look
back on in order to understand your feelings
about certain people, places and situations.
Try focusing your diary entries on positive and
negative feelings; ask yourself where and when
you feel happiest, where you feel uncomfortable
and who affects your mood. Be honest with
yourself and use this as a learning tool.

Start your diary-writing journey here. Include what you want to get out of writing a diary and how you think it will benefit you. In order to gain greater insight into your thoughts and emotions, include both positive and negative feelings.

Dear diary,

...................................................................................................
...................................................................................................
...................................................................................................
...................................................................................................
...................................................................................................
...................................................................................................
...................................................................................................
...................................................................................................
...................................................................................................
...................................................................................................
...................................................................................................
...................................................................................................
...................................................................................................
...................................................................................................
...................................................................................................
...................................................................................................
...................................................................................................
...................................................................................................

# Use this space to write your own thoughts.

# STAY BALANCED

A well-balanced diet is essential for providing the
energy you need to stay active. There are many physical
health benefits to eating well. Studies have also shown
that there are links between healthy eating and better
moods, with people being happier and less depressed.
The most important thing to bear in mind when trying
to adopt a healthy eating plan is to start with a balanced
diet that incorporates all the major food groups.
Once you have ensured that you are getting enough
protein, fibre, fat and plenty of vitamin-rich fruits and
vegetables, you have a great starting point. If you are
unsure of which foods are best for optimum health,
a web search will provide you with comprehensive
lists of foods rich in the nutrients you require,
allowing you to plan healthier meals for
your personal dietary requirements.

Do some research into balanced diets and write a list of foods rich in the nutrients your body requires.

- .................................................
- .................................................
- .................................................

- .................................................
- .................................................
- .................................................

Use the planner below to schedule a week of healthy meals using your list for inspiration.

|  | Breakfast | Lunch | Dinner | Snacks |
|---|---|---|---|---|
| MON |  |  |  |  |
| TUE |  |  |  |  |
| WED |  |  |  |  |
| THU |  |  |  |  |
| FRI |  |  |  |  |
| SAT |  |  |  |  |
| SUN |  |  |  |  |

# Use this space to write your own thoughts.

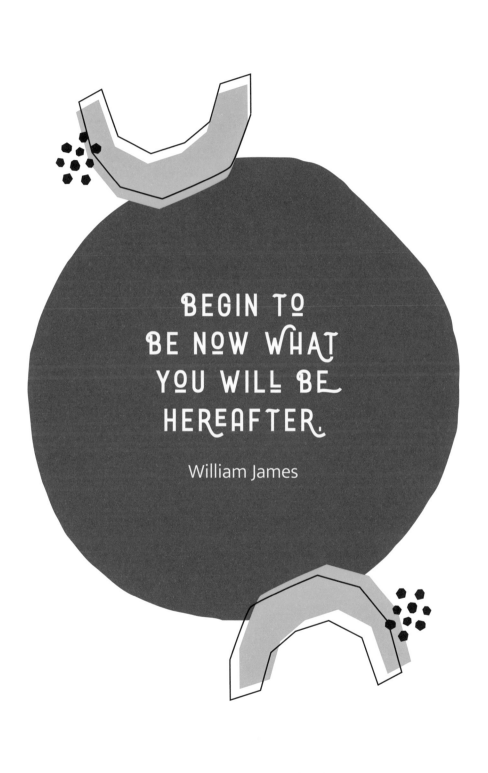

BEGIN TO
BE NOW WHAT
YOU WILL BE
HEREAFTER.

William James

# BE ACE

Low mood can make the body feel stressed, and high levels of stress hormones in your system can have a negative effect on your health, either by lowering your immune system or by overstimulating it and provoking autoimmune illnesses and inflammation. A simple way to combat these symptoms is to eat plenty of foods rich in the antioxidant vitamins A, C and E. Vitamin A is found in products such as fish livers and oils, and egg yolks. Too much retinol can be bad for your health, though, so balance this with beta carotene, mainly found in yellow and orange fruits and vegetables such as carrots, butternut squash and apricots. Vitamin C is found in good amounts in citrus fruits, broccoli, berries and tomatoes, and vitamin E is found in nuts, seeds, avocados, olive oil and wheatgerm. Adding some of these foods to your diet could make you feel healthier and happier, a great combination for positivity!

**Write a list of long-term health goals you want to achieve, along with a time frame for achieving them.**

- ...........................................................................................................
- ...........................................................................................................
- ...........................................................................................................
- ...........................................................................................................

What is your motivation for being healthier?

...........................................................................................................

...........................................................................................................

...........................................................................................................

...........................................................................................................

...........................................................................................................

In the space below, describe the first simple steps you could take towards a healthier lifestyle.

...........................................................................................................

...........................................................................................................

...........................................................................................................

...........................................................................................................

...........................................................................................................

Use this space to write your own thoughts.

# B POSITIVE

B vitamins are particularly important for maintaining a positive mood and therefore for feeling good. Among their many functions, B vitamins are involved in the body's control of tryptophan, a building block for serotonin. Vitamin B6 is essential in the production of GABA (gamma-aminobutyric acid), which helps boost mood in a similar way to serotonin. A lack of these neurotransmitters can lead to low mood, which in turn can lead to serious psychological problems, such as depression. The main vitamins to pay attention to are B1, B2, B3, B5, B6, B9 and B12, all of which can be found in a balanced diet. If you eat a lot of processed foods or are vegan, you may be lacking in certain B vitamins, in which case adding a B-vitamin supplement to your diet can have an excellent effect on your overall health and mood.

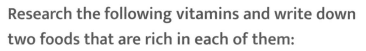

**Research the following vitamins and write down two foods that are rich in each of them:**

**B1**
...............................................................................................

**B2**
...............................................................................................

**B3**
...............................................................................................

**B5**
...............................................................................................

**B6**
...............................................................................................

**B9**
...............................................................................................

**B12**
...............................................................................................

Are there any foods that you find can lead to a low mood after eating them?

...............................................................................................

...............................................................................................

...............................................................................................

What are the physical and mental benefits you experience when eating healthily?

...............................................................................................

...............................................................................................

...............................................................................................

...............................................................................................

...............................................................................................

Use this space to write your own thoughts.

GOOD
THINGS
ARE
COMING
MY WAY

# USE SUPPLEMENTS

Mood changes are often due to imbalances in your body. As an extra way to keep your mood positive, supplements can be very helpful when used in addition to a balanced and healthy lifestyle. If you talk to someone at your local health food shop or natural pharmacy, they will be able to give you advice on what is best for you, personally. The herbal supplements that are most likely to help you stay positive are those that help boost the mood and reduce stress, for example 5-HTP (5-hydroxytryptophan), which helps to boost natural serotonin levels, or passiflora (passion flower), which helps promote calm and sleep. These are widely available, as are many other beneficial supplements.

Do some research into different supplements that boost your mood and reduce stress that are available from your local health food shop or natural pharmacy. Document their names and their health benefits in the space below. Before taking any supplements, discuss with a trained professional.

........................................................................
........................................................................
........................................................................
........................................................................
........................................................................
........................................................................
........................................................................
........................................................................
........................................................................
........................................................................
........................................................................
........................................................................
........................................................................
........................................................................
........................................................................
........................................................................

**Use this space to write your own thoughts.**

# LEARN HOW MUCH SLEEP YOU NEED

We are told that the average adult needs eight hours of sleep each night, but we are not all average. Knowing what is normal for you can help you to be sure that you are not oversleeping or getting too little sleep, either of which can be a source of concern. It may help to keep a sleep diary, or to use an app that tells you the optimum time to wake up, taking into consideration your chosen bedtime (though of course, it's best not to look at the app too close to bedtime). Many apps give several options based on the number of full sleep cycles you require. Changing our perceptions of the amount we need to sleep can help us to feel more secure and therefore help us sleep more easily, which leaves us more rested and ready to take on new challenges with a positive outlook.

Complete a sleep diary for a week to
see how much sleep you are getting.

|  | Sleep time | Wake time | Quality of sleep (1–10) | Total number of hours asleep | How did you feel the day after? |
|---|---|---|---|---|---|
| MON | | | | | |
| TUE | | | | | |
| WED | | | | | |
| THU | | | | | |
| FRI | | | | | |
| SAT | | | | | |
| SUN | | | | | |

What did you notice about the amount of sleep
you got and how you felt the next day? Write your
thoughts and findings in the space below.

......................................................................................................

......................................................................................................

**Use this space to write your own thoughts.**

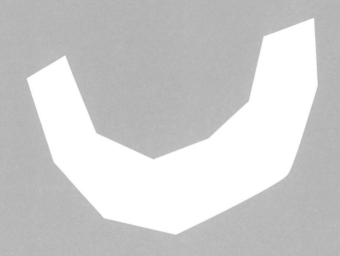

SOMETIMES THE
SMALLEST STEP IN
THE RIGHT DIRECTION
ENDS UP BEING
THE BIGGEST STEP
OF YOUR LIFE.

Naeem Callaway

# IMPROVE YOUR ENERGY WITH REIKI

Reiki is an energy practice that works in a similar way to massage or acupressure. In reiki, however, the therapist will usually not make direct contact with you; rather, they will hold their hands a short distance from your body in certain areas in order to massage your energy field. Reiki practitioners believe that we not only have energy flowing through our bodies, but that this energy is palpable in a field outside of ourselves, and that, using this field, they can improve mood disturbances and heal illnesses. Why not seek out a reiki therapist at your local natural health centre, or online.

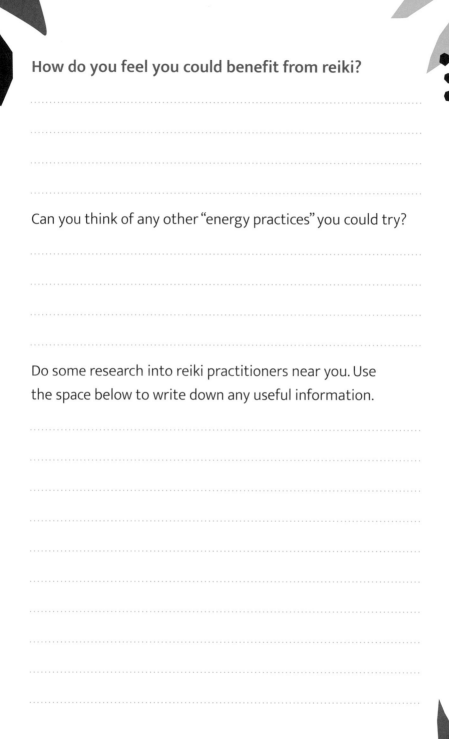

## How do you feel you could benefit from reiki?

.................................................................................

.................................................................................

.................................................................................

.................................................................................

Can you think of any other "energy practices" you could try?

.................................................................................

.................................................................................

.................................................................................

.................................................................................

Do some research into reiki practitioners near you. Use
the space below to write down any useful information.

.................................................................................

.................................................................................

.................................................................................

.................................................................................

.................................................................................

.................................................................................

.................................................................................

.................................................................................

.................................................................................

.................................................................................

.................................................................................

## Use this space to write your own thoughts.

# RELAX STEP BY STEP

Both meditation and yoga teach us that progressive relaxation, a technique that involves tensing and relaxing your muscles, is an excellent way to aid sleep. It is often the case that when low mood strikes and we feel negative, we lie awake at night unable to relax. This simple exercise will help you to relax your body and ease your mind in preparation for a good night's sleep. Concentrating on each body part at a time, start at your feet and work your way up your body. For each body part, clench it as tightly as you can before letting it go, feeling the physical relaxation that comes with this release. Some people find it helpful to use a verbal aid, for example, saying or thinking "I am relaxing my feet; my feet are now completely relaxed", and repeating for each body part.

**Perform the bedtime relaxation activity on the previous page and when you have finished complete the task below.**

On the diagram, colour in the areas of your body that felt most relaxed.

Using a different colour, fill any areas you felt tension or pain.

In the space below, describe the effects this relaxation technique had on your mind and body.

.................................................

.................................................

.................................................

.................................................

.................................................

.................................................

.................................................

.................................................

.................................................

.................................................

.................................................

## Use this space to write your own thoughts.

I WILL NOT
WORRY ABOUT
TOMORROW,
I WILL
EMBRACE
TODAY

# INDULGE IN AROMATHERAPY

Aromatherapy uses essential oils from plants to help calm or stimulate the mind and body. To keep your mood positive, try using stimulating oils such as geranium, rosemary or peppermint, or uplifting scents such as rose, bergamot or neroli. These can be used traditionally for massage, steam inhalation or as bath oils, but they can also be used around your home or workplace to help bring your mood up throughout the day. Try sprinkling some drops on a pomander to put in a drawer with your clothes, or using your favourite oil on some unscented potpourri. You can also get roll-on essential oils, which you use in a similar way to perfumes, putting them on your wrist where the warmth will disperse the uplifting scent around you all day.

Find somewhere you can test some essential oils. Write the names of the oils and any words that your mind conjures up in association with the scent.

How could you introduce aromatherapy into your life?

..................................................................................................

..................................................................................................

Describe a time when scent has evoked strong, positive memories.

..................................................................................................

..................................................................................................

Use this space to write your own thoughts.

# AND FINALLY...
# SEE YOUR DOCTOR

Although the tips in this book can help you stay positive, if you feel that negativity has taken over your life in an unhealthy way and is having a detrimental effect on your health, the best advice is to consult with your doctor. Negativity and low mood can be signs of more serious underlying conditions and your doctor may suggest a talking therapy such as CBT, or the use of medication, to get you back to where you want to be.

**Write a list of people, along with their contact details, that you can always call upon for support.**

- .............................................................................................................
- .............................................................................................................
- .............................................................................................................
- .............................................................................................................
- .............................................................................................................
- .............................................................................................................
- .............................................................................................................
- .............................................................................................................

Use the internet to do some research into talking therapy charities near you. In the space below, write down contact details for when, if ever, you should need them.

.............................................................................................................

.............................................................................................................

.............................................................................................................

.............................................................................................................

.............................................................................................................

.............................................................................................................

.............................................................................................................

Use this space to write your own thoughts.

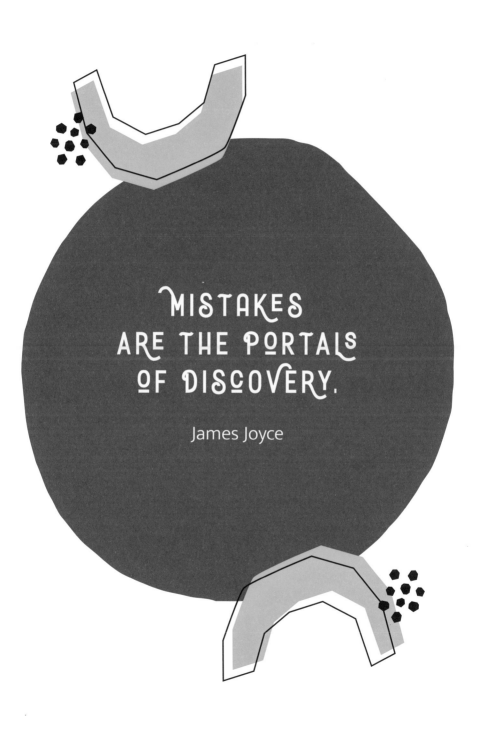

MISTAKES
ARE THE PORTALS
OF DISCOVERY.

James Joyce

# FINAL WORD

Congratulations for completing this positivity journal. Positivity is about maintaining an optimistic outlook on life in times of challenge and adversity, so endeavour to use the tools within this book to continue to seek out and discover joy and contentment. Positivity is the key to well-being; when you feel positive about yourself, the path to health and happiness becomes so much easier.

If you find yourself slipping back into negativity, look back through your journal revisiting the key points in which you identify your strengths and motivations to attune yourself to a more positive, happier state.

Self-care is an essential part of being able to maintain positivity, so remember to take time to rest and recharge your batteries. It is harder to maintain a positive mental attitude if you're running on empty. Remember there are a number of great ways to help maintain your positivity. Exercise can help reduce anxiety, healthy eating can boost brain function and progressive relaxation is a great way to aid sleep, all significantly contributing to your health and emotional well-being.

### Happiness for Every Day Journal

**Simple Tips and Guided Exercises to Help You Find Joy**

Paperback

ISBN: 978-1-80007-832-1

### Mindfulness for Every Day Journal

**Simple Tips and Guided Exercises to Help You Live in the Moment**

Paperback

ISBN: 978-1-80007-835-2

### Resilience for Every Day Journal

**Simple Tips and Guided Exercises to Help You Find Your Inner Strength**

Paperback

ISBN: 978-1-80007-834-5

Have you enjoyed this book?
If so, find us on Facebook at **Summersdale
Publishers**, on Twitter at **@Summersdale** and
on Instagram at **@summersdalebooks** and
get in touch. We'd love to hear from you!

**www.summersdale.com**

## IMAGE CREDITS